Faithful Father, Forever Friend

ALICE JANE STUCKEY

ISBN 978-1-64569-206-5 (paperback)
ISBN 978-1-64569-207-2 (digital)

Christian Faith Publishing, Inc.
832 Park Avenue
Meadville, PA 16335
www.christianfaithpublishing.com

Printed in the United States of America

If we are not faithful, he will still be faithful,
because he must be true to who he is

—2 Timothy 2:13–15, NCV

I cannot remember a time when I did not know who God or Jesus was. Grandma and Daddy took the three of us girls to Sunday school and church every Sunday morning. Grandma played the hymns on our old piano. She read her Bible and listened to Rex Humbard.

Before our meals, we prayed, "Thank you for the world so sweet. Thank you for the food we eat. Thank you for the birds that sing. Thank you, God, for everything."

At night, before we went to bed, we bowed our heads, folded our hands, and prayed, "Now I lay me down to sleep. I pray the Lord, my soul to keep. If I should die before I wake, I pray the Lord, my soul to take."

But did I know God? Did I know him personally? Was he real to me or only a historical person I had read about in that big book called the Bible? I knew all the right answers when questioned, just as I did when quizzed about George Washington or Abraham Lincoln. I believed Washington and Lincoln were real for I had read about them in a book, but I had no personal relationship with either of them. Neither did I have a personal relationship with God.

This is my journey of friendship with the one true God. God has proven himself to be my faithful Father—my forever friend.

Woman uses poetry to record important events

Alice Jane Stuckey uses poetry to record many of the important events of her life.

When she was in the eighth grade, the teacher asked the pupils to write original poems as part of the English assignment. Unlike some of her classmates, Alice enjoyed the assignment.

"I found that it was an easy thing for me to do. There were so many things happening in my life at that time that the words just seemed to flow out of my pen," she says. "The next day the teacher called me to her desk and asked how long I had been doing poetry.

"Of course I hadn't been writing anything of a poetic sense before that, but after that, whenever I wanted to write about something that happened, I did it in a poetic way. I could let out my feelings that way as well," she says.

Some of her poems have been published after being submitted in contests. Others have been used by clubs and other organizations.

Alice Jane Risdon was born May 16, 1950, in Sandusky to Glenn and Pearl Risdon. Her family, which lived in Vermilion, included two older sisters and two brothers, who died when they were very young.

Alice lost her mother at age 3 and

Now... and then
By Jean Walek

went to live with her grandmother along with her two sisters. Grandma became the center of Alice's world. The one who kissed the hurts to make them well, who called them to come for meals, washed their hands and faces. Later, Grandma would tuck them into bed and tell them interesting bedtime stories.

After more than six years at Grandma's, father married again, and Alice moved back home. It took a time for adjustments between the 9-year-old and a stepmother, but Alice and Edna are now friends.

Alice graduated from school in Vermilion in June 1968.

Her first full-time job was on the assembly line at the Norwalk Westinghouse plant. The plant, which has since closed, is where she met that great guy who would mean so much in her life, William A. Stuckey.

Alice and Bill started dating in September 1968 and were married on March 29, 1969. To their union came a son Brian, who is now grown and working in Norwalk.

In poetic form, Alice describes her delight at his birth, of his progress through the early years, of going off to school for the first time, of learning and of helping.

One poem describes young Brian, along with his mother who was sick with the flu. It recalls how he tried to help by bringing her a glass of water and by playing quietly by her bed as she slept. He even tried to sweep the floor. It is a poem about a good little boy trying to be the man of the house until daddy comes home.

Alice preferred to be a full-time wife and mother for about 10 years after Brian's birth. She she worked as a bookkeeper, cost accountant, saleswoman, secretary and receptionist.

Alice Jane Stuckey has been writing poetry since the eighth-grade. (Reflector photo by Peter Fellman)

Bill operates an insurance agency out of their home, and Alice also helps out with much of the book work. They also have five acres with their home on Shawmill Road and use some of it for crops.

The poem "My Tractor" describes her thoughts as she is driving over the field, feeling the power of the machine. She expresses the freedom she feels and expresses an outpouring of thanks to God for listening as she speaks to Him.

Bill spends a great deal of time with his business, and with both working, it is sometimes difficult to

take time off. Alice does crocheting in quiet times and helps Bill with his stamp collection. She is also very involved with her church and has been a Sunday school teacher for a long time.

Working as a bookkeeper at a discount drug store on the north side of town lets her have the contact with people she likes. She continues to carry a notepad in her purse so that she can write down a line or a verse as it comes to her.

"I hope some day to be able to put them in book form so that I can share them with others," she says.

Recording my friendship with God, began with a
single writing assignment in eighth grade.

Contents

Growing Pains

Spiritual Comfort

Poems on Death

Poems on Depression

1

Christian Life Poems

A Way of Life

He stood in the pulpit
And preached the Word.
(One of the best preachers
I've ever heard!)
He sang in a voice
So deep and low.
I doubt there was a song
He did not know!
He and his wife
Sang in a quartet
Spreading God's love
To those that they met.
A treasured hug
A word of cheer
A word of wisdom
To dry a tear!
Unlike many
Who preached for a living
Instead of taking
I found him giving!
I would see those who set hours
From nine to five
Thinking their congregation
Could survive.
But daily contact
Was what was needed
And that's why this brother
Had succeeded.

By his side
A dedicated wife.
Preaching wasn't a job
But a way of life!

He sang in a voice so deep and low. I doubt
there was a song he did not know.

Analyzed Writing

Can you analyze my writing?
Do you know who I really am?
Do you only view the surface?
Or do you see deep within?
My poems tell the story
Of a simple person's life.
They reveal the true feeling
Of mother, daughter, wife.
They let you see the person
Who walks beside you every day
And help you understand
The things I do and say.
I don't mean to offend you
Or rub a raw nerve
I only hope you'll understand me
And allow me to serve.

At the Master's Feet

To be like Mary
At the Master's feet
Never too busy
To take a seat.
Worldly demands
Lure me away.
But 'tis at my Lord's feet
That I want to stay.
But like Martha
I am often pulled away
By the many duties
Of each passing day.
The dishes need washing
And the meals need cooking.
My once empty schedule
Is now overbooked.
The floors need sweeping
And the errands need ran.
I'm doing the best
I possibly can!
Slow me down, Lord
Just for today.
'Tis at your feet
I'm longing to stay!

Bends in the Road

Life is full of so many bends. We go along so long on the straight road. Then suddenly ahead we see our path is about to change. We approach the curves with apprehension, wondering what lies beyond. We feel a tinge of excitement, mixed with fear of the unknown.

Sometimes, we come to a *Y* in the road and have a choice to make. So many decisions—so many questions of what will be best—not only for me, but others; not only for now, but later.

Many times we rise up the steep mountains of challenges and success, or we slide down into the valleys and dales of uncertainty and fears.

As we travel these uncharted waters, let us bear in mind: the Lord of the universe is in control, and in his omniscience, he knows where each road leads.

Betrayed

As they went to the garden
To pray and reminisce
Who would have thought
He'd be betrayed by a kiss?
And who would have thought
The friends by his side
Would be found sleeping
As he knelt there and cried?
Who would have thought
When his deepest need came
Those whom he loved
Would deny his name?
I stand here in awe
When I see how I live
That he's raising his eyes
Saying, "Father, forgive."

Building Blocks

Building blocks of the Church
Father, Mother, Sister, Brother
All one big family
Loving one another.
Should one block deteriorate
And crumble in the wall
Would we pick our brother up
Or let the building fall?
It takes every two by four
To make our building strong.
If we leave one cracked or broken
We're doing something wrong!

Busyness

Busy lives
And busy days.
All are running
Different ways.
Never slowing down
One bit.
Never a moment
Just to sit!

Ceiling Tile in the Church Building

Have you ever glanced upward while you sat in the church building? The ceiling tiles have a message for me. Each little square represents a congregation—a part of the body of Christ. One square I call Norwalk, Ohio. Another square is Madison, Alabama. Another is Punxsutawney, Pennsylvania. Another is Amherst, New London, Bellevue, Sandusky, Vermilion, or Perth, Scotland.

All of these squares are connected together to make one ceiling, as each of the congregations make one church.

Inside each square, I see dark, thick lines and soft little dots. The thick lines in the congregation are the stronger members. They stand out more. The dots are the weaker members. They tend to fade into the background.

I'd like to be one of those strong, thick lines who stands out for Christ. I'd like to be in a congregation touching others, instead of a ceiling tile, alone, without a ceiling.

As I look at the ceiling and imagine each block a congregation of my Lord's church, it amazes me. When I think of each tile in that ceiling having so many members, it astounds me. How blessed I am to have such a family!

Does God Demand an Apology?

Does God demand an apology
The way I do my child?
Does he sit and fuss and fume
And make him stew a while?
Does he refuse to hear his pleas
And let his child doubt?
When his child returns to him
Does he throw his child out?
Or is he waiting, as I have heard
With his arms spread wide and open?
Knowing we're sorry for our offense
Before the words have yet been spoken?

Eyes on Jesus

Eyes on Jesus
And off the world
Eyes on Jesus
My soul be filled.
Sometimes I worry
Sometimes I fret.
Eye off Jesus
I get upset.
When I begin
To look at man
See greed and hate
On every hand
My heart grows sad
By what I see.
Eyes on Jesus
Not on me!
Oft I'm tempted
To look about:
Eyes off Jesus
I start to doubt.
Turn to Jesus
And trust in his will.
Eyes on Jesus
Oh, heart, be still!

God Has Big Plans for Me!

God has big plans for me.
Although I may not see
Just what he has in store
He'll open up a door.
If I'll but trust his grace
He'll guide me in the race.
Through mountains steep and valleys low
He'll lead me as I onward go.
If I wait patiently
I'll see his plan for me.
Following his will—not mine
I'll cross the victory line.
I will not curse my fate
But follow through the gate.
For what now seems a mystery
Is just part of God's
Big plans for me!

God Knows Best

When I look back across my life
And see where God has led
Then it's easier to understand
The present can't be bad.
I strike against what I do not know.
I fight what I cannot see.
But deep down in my heart, I know
God knows what's best for me!

God of Love

I can feel God's presence
through your friendship.
When I am happy
You are happy for me.
And when I am sad
You are there to hold my hand.
When I am tempted to do wrong
You give sound advice.
When I am blinded to my good points
You show me where they lie.
Thank you for showing me
A God of love!

God the Parent

Just when I think
I cannot go on
He leads to Calvary
And his dying son.
He reminds me, he too
Is a parent, like me
And doing what's right
Isn't always easy.
That sometimes we must let
Our sons suffer alone
For when they are men
They have missions of their own!

Guard Me, God

Guard my tongue, oh God
And check each passing word.
May I repeat only the good
Of all the things I've heard.
Guard my eyes, oh God
And help me to be blind
To other's irritating ways
And when they lag behind.
Guard my hands, oh, God
And keep them busy for the Lord.
There is so much I have to do
That idleness I can't afford.
Guard thou my entire being
As I go about my tasks each day.
Guard me with thine eye—all seeing.
In thy loving arms, let me ever stay!

I've Found God

I've found God upon the mountain
Away from worldly noise.
I've left the world behind me
To glimpse at heaven's joys.
I've feasted on the fellowship
Of brothers joined together
To feel the love and joy and peace
To think that heaven's better!
Yes, I've found God upon the mountain
In the people that I've met
And as I strive for heaven's goal
I never shall forget!

Life's Jewels

Precious stones
Of daily living.
Unnoticed blessings
God keeps giving.
A simple smile
A nod "Hello,"
A card in the mail
Saying, "I want you to know."
An invitation
"Come over and talk."
Sighting gems
On a springtime walk.
A hot cup of coffee
My Bible in hand.
A day to relax
Where nothing is planned.
Pondering what lies
Beyond the azure-blue sky
Where someday I'll live
With Jesus on high!

Little Boy Grown

Who is that gentleman?
Who is that Godly man
Who is his trusted friend?
What makes his faith so strong?
Who gives his heart a song?
Faithful, though things go wrong?
Trusting his Lord and king.
Faithful in the good times
And the bad times too.
Faithful to my Jesus.
He will see me through.
Faithful in the sunshine
And when the clouds appear.
Trusting that he'll be mine
Though sight is blocked by tears.

Loving Jesus

In the scheme of things
This world is hard.
We feel the pain and stings
Of a life that is hard.
If this was all
Life had to give
We'd surely fall.
We should not live.
God did not leave us
Here to die.
Without purpose
To question why.
God has a plan
For each of us.
Loving Jesus
Is a must!
Because he lived
And died for me.
Heaven's home
My eternity.

Mary's Lamb

Mary had a little lamb
He was born in a stable.
He came to earth to save our souls
Because we were not able.
Mary's little boy
Grew up to be a man
And he was tempted in every way
Just the way I am!
Now, I don't have to walk alone
He suffered on that tree.
Mary's little lamb bled and died
Because of you and me.

Mary's Lamb II

Mary had a little lamb
He washed me white as snow.
Now Mary's lamb goes with me
Everywhere I go.
He followed me to work one day
Which wasn't quite the rule.
He saw some things I had to say
Were really mean and cruel.
We cannot leave the lamb at home
And go to work all day
For Satan's always on the prowl
Stalking out his prey.
It breaks my heart to have God see
The way I really am.
I must confess; I am the one.
I murdered Mary's lamb!

Masks

I remove my mask
For all to see
The hurt; the love
Inside of me.
I refuse to hide
Even one small spot.
I won't have you believing
What I am not.
If I remove my mask
'Tis no big deal.
For all you see
Is what is real.
And if I remove
My mask for you
Perhaps you would
Remove yours too.
Then, I can love you
And you can love me
And not just someone
We pretend to be.

Meditation

Help me, Lord, to appreciate
The time you give to meditate.
When I am stuck in a traffic jam
Help me to dwell on Christ, the lamb.
When I find my days are long
Help me, Lord, to praise in song.
When I feel that life can't wait
That's when I need to meditate!

My Light

Let the work of my hands
Bear witness to him.
May my light ever shine?
And never grow dim!
When I am tempted
To grumble or shout
May his word in my heart
Fight the darkness and doubt!
When I'm tempted
To go with the crowd
Let me first ask
Would my Father be proud?
When I am tempted
To be lax like the rest
Remind me, 'tis for God
That I do my best.
When the lights burn low
And things seem grim
Let the works of my hands
Bring glory to him!

My Tractor

My tractor is my quiet place
For God and me alone.
'Tis where I meet him face to face
And bow before his throne.
I pour my troubles out to him.
I sing his praise out loud.
I tell him of my every whim.
I shout it to the clouds.
No one hears, but God and me
As round the field I go.
I hand him all my agony
While driving down the row.

My tractor is my hiding place for me and God alone.

Never-Changing Love

I thank you, God
When I forget.
You are faithful to me.
You do not quit.
You fill in the void
When I feel the lack.
You gently love me
Coaxing me back.
You remind me
When I feel alone
It was for my sins
You did atone.
Nothing can come
Between the two of us.
God's never-changing love
I what I can trust!

Pausing on the Jericho Road

Have you dared to pause on the Jericho Road
To aid a traveler in need?
As you passed the weary, have you stopped
To plant that first little seed?
Have you taken the time from your busy schedule?
To offer a helping hand?
Have you bent to remove the shoes from their feet?
To shake out the pebbles of sand?
The Lord hasn't placed you on the Jericho Road
Just to enjoy the great view.
There's a harvest to gather; there's work to be done
And he knows the workers are few!
We've just a few days to share in God's praise
And pint the way to the door
So row up your sleeves before the season is past
And the reaping shall be no more.

Saving Grace

I do not deny the hardships.
I do not deny the truth.
I simply know that God is.
My life is living proof.
He loved my little timid soul
Through those who knew him well.
He groomed me with their tender love
And rescued me from hell.
Had they not walked the rocky road
Handling their sin and strife
They could not have touched this little soul
And brought it back to life.
Help me, dear Lord, to be aware
How much you've done for me.
So when others look my way, dear Lord
Your grace is all they see!

So What?

Deep in thought
My husband sits
I talk to him
But he forgets!
So what?
Bills are always
Here to pay.
We haven't money
For that today!
So what?
I'm always prompt
He's always late.
I hate it when
He procrastinates!
So what?
A misunderstanding
A rude word spoken
A rough kid comes
A toy is broken!
So what?
The wash isn't done.
The beds aren't made.
Supper's done
But my husband's late!
So what?
And what does it matter
If I don't agree
With the person

Sitting next to me?
So what?
What if someone
Tires to used me?
Feelings hurt
When they abuse me!
So what?
Someone forgets me
Doesn't call
Then my spirits
Start to fall!
So what?
The old get slow
My patience grows thin
Forgetting someday
I may be like him!
So what?
So what?
These things won't matter
In the end
When before the Lord
I stand!
So let me
Think and speak and act
Kindly, loving
And with tact!
These things will all be washed away
When I face the judgment day.
So what should matter most to me
Is where I spend eternity!

Son Shine

The sun shines down on me
And warms the earth around.
I hear the song birds in the air
They make the sweetest sound.
The clouds send forth refreshing rains.
The trees sway in the breeze.
The beauty of creation bends me low
In thanksgiving to my knees.
The same Son who shines on me
Shines also down on you.
He bids you come before his throne
Because he loves you too!

Spiritual DNA

Fires purify us
Bring impurities to the surface.
Though we may not realize
Trials have a purpose.
Trials are not pleasant.
The process seems so slow.
But facing them with Jesus
Enables us to grow.
If it were not for the testing
That God has brought my way
I may have never realized
My spiritual DNA.

Standing before the Judge

I stood there in the courtroom
And knew that eyes were fixed on me.
I felt a heaviness and doom
As I entered a "no contest" plea.
I knew that I was guilty
And my deeds had sealed my fate.
I'd run recklessly on thru life
And now it was too late.
It always happened to someone else.
I would not be caught.
But there I stood before the judge
And he could not be bought!
I stood to hear the verdict
In trembling and fear.
I did not want to face the words
I knew that I must hear.
"Not guilty!" was the judgment
I heard my Savior give
"Her slate has been wiped clean;
I died that she might live!"

Staying with the Ship

Have you cut your lifeboat loose?
Are you staying with the ship?
Or are you clinging to the side
For fear you'll fall and slip?
The Lord has promised safety
Upon life's stormy sea.
He's said, "Come ye heavy laden,"
"Come ye unto me."
He'll never send us trials
More than we can bear.
As long as we stay with the ship
We're in the Father's care!

The Birthday Cake

It was just a cake
An ordinary cake.
No special ingredients
In what he planned to bake!
It took little effort
Just a bit of time
Only cost bout two dollars
And maybe one more dime.
'Twas just a birthday cake
That he'd taken to the shut-in.
But you should have seen her smile
You should have seen her grin!
It makes a world of difference
When we give our love away
For the fact that he remembered
Brightened her whole day!

It was just a cake.

The Great Caregiver

I care for you
And do what I can.
But the Great Caregiver
Is the great, "I am."
In prayer for you
I lift you to God
As daily I strive
His pathway to trod.
Though my hands are weak
And sometimes I fail
I know that through Christ
His love will prevail.
I must remember
You were just here on loan
And the Great Caregiver
Has beckoned you home!
Your caregiver loves you
And will bring sweet release.
For the great, "I am,"
Is the Prince of Peace!

The House beside the Road

It was just a house beside the road
That the stranger had walked down.
He stood outside in the cold
Upon his face a sullen frown.
Through the windows, he could see
People going here and there
A warm and loving family
And Father in the rocking chair.
He longed to step in through the door
And steal the warmth that this house held.
He yearned to grasp a little more
For God's love, he beheld!
And just as he turned to go
The door flung open wide.
"No need to stay out in the shadow,"
"Won't you please come inside?"
There are many lurking round
Standing out there in the cold.
May it be my house they've found
An open door beside the road.

It was just a house beside the road.

The Olive Root

Don't sever me from the Olive Tree
From the Root that's buried below.
'Tis the source of life for me
The manna to my soul.
Since I've been grafted to the Tree
By the blood of the Savior divine
I've found a strength that's not in me.
I am the Lord's and he is mine.
T'would I be severed from the Olive Root
My branch would wither and die
And I would miss an eternity
In my heavenly home on high.

The Path Maker

You are my leader.
You are my guide
You are my God
Walking close by my side.
You go ahead of me.
A light on my way.
You pilot me when skies are blue
And, also, when skies are gray.
You take me on a safer route
When I open up your book.
I'd avoid so many dangers
If I'd only take a look!
You cut away the stubble
And weeds that block my path.
I lean upon your word, O God
Your mighty, stable staff.

The Potter's Clay

A little bit of kindness
Sprinkled along the way
Has been known to soften hearts
And mold them, just like clay.
For clay along the murky banks
Will always be just clay
'Til the potter picks it up
And fashions it his way.
And so it is with kindness
As we give ourselves away
We form a lovely vessel
As the potter does the clay!

The Savior's Face

Our days are so filled with business
That we seldom stop to think
Jesus may be standing at our door
Begging us for a drink!
We go about our daily tasks
With so much eagerness and speed
We fail to stop and recognize
The other person's need.
If only I could put myself
In the hungry child's place
Then, maybe, when she came by knocking
I could see my Savior's face.

The Savior's Love

If all he had to do
Was leave his home above
That would have been enough
To prove the Savior's love.
But he did much more
Than leave his heavenly throne
When he came down
To make this earth his home.
He walked the places
That we walk.
He heard the talk
That we talk.
He felt our pain
He felt our grief.
He left his home
To bring relief.
He suffered rejection
Pain and loss.
Alone he hung
Upon the cross.
A loving Savior
Such as he
Deserves the best
From you and me!

The Seat Reserved for Me

The big day is coming.
Invitations are being sent.
We're all anticipating.
That glorious event!
Reservations have been made
And a seat's awaiting me
For when we accept our Savior
He checks RSVP.
My chair's reserved in heaven
And no one can take my place
For it was granted me
By the Father's heavenly grace!
How sad t'will be to see
Just one empty chair
For when I get to heaven
I want all my family there!

Twists in the Road

The road I travel twists and turns
And leads me through a foreign land.
It takes me places I'd dare not go
If the Master weren't holding my hand.
Often the road seems long and rough
The hills too steep to climb.
I grow weary and sit myself down
Forgetting he's there all the time.
But when I fix my eyes on him
I need not run and hide.
For I can conquer the hurdles of life
With Jesus as my guide!

Walking on the Water

Like Peter
When the challenge came
I stepped out in faith
When I heard my name.
I forged ahead
Upon the stream
Facing adventure
Grasping a dream.
But all too soon
My eyes looked down
And when I fumbled
I thought I'd drown.
I searched desperately
For dry land
Forgetting to take
The Master's hand.
But once again
I heard him say
"Trust in me
I am the way."

Wealth

Money in the bank.
Cars in the yard.
How can I forget to thank
The one and only God?
Things that mean so much to me
I will not give away.
But when I enter eternity
These things will have to stay.
Blessings from the Father's hand
Are not for me to hoard.
They paint a picture where I stand
In relation to my Lord.
Will I simply use them on myself?
Forgetting why you came?
No I will used my worldly wealth
To glorify your name!

Ziklag

Even though Ziklag lay in ruins
My Lord still reigns on high.
There is naught for me to fear
For God is ever neigh!
Though sin's smoke has blocked the Son
And my way's grown dark and dreary
The Father patiently awaits the return
Of all the worn and weary.
My Ziklag may stand ablaze
With fire raging round me
But I am safe, what err befall
Since Jesus came and found me!
—1 Samuel 30:1–6

2

Growing Pains

Alice?

Alice?
I knew her long ago.
(At least, I thought I did!)
Now, at times
I doubt it so.
(Memories as a kid!)
Alice
A little girl with hair in braids
Running around the farm.
Oh, so often
Memory fades
It causes me alarm!
Alice
When asked
Whose girl she was
She replied
"Everybody's," because
She didn't want to take sides. Alice?
With a listening ear
To another's cares and woes.
But, now, Alice does not hear.
She's deaf to those she knows.
Alice went through so many
Seasons in her life.

Daughter, sister
mother, wife.
Alice grew throughout
the years.
Alice cried
so many tears.
Alice now knows
these were growing pains.
Nothing ventured
Nothing gained.
She had to struggle
search and pray.
But God was with her
every day.

A little girl with hair in braids, running around the farm.

Anger's Bomb

Like a bomb
Ready to explode
I feel the seconds tick.
Alarming tension
All around
As shorter grows the wick!
Frantically
I search in vain
The end of the fuse
Trying hard to stop it's flame
But it's no use.
Anger swells
Within my breast
Leaving my heart cold.
Unceasingly, I probe for love
Least forgiveness
I withhold.
Resentment grows
To full-scale size
Smothering me to death.
Bitterness chokes my heart
Causing
My last breath.
There is so much missing
Deep inside
When we shut the door on him
But, oh, how hard
Satan cried
When I bid my Savior in!

Christian Charity

I didn't mean to grumble
'Bout the man who wore his welcome out
Nor did I see it as being mean
When I shunned the man who was unclean.
Until the day that my turn came
And I was treated just the same.
The guilt within my heart ran deep
As it stole away much-needed sleep.
Now I knew how it felt to be
Shunned by Christian charity!

Christs Sweet Home

There was a time
(I remember when)
Not long ago
I had no friend.
When trials piled
And were hard to bear
I would not permit
Another's care.
I built a barrier
Between you and me
For fear of the person
I knew you'd see.
But you opened your heart
And bid me come in
That I might see Christ
And better know him.
We need never carry
Our burdens alone
For in the hearts
Of his loved ones
He makes
His sweet home!

Everybody's Little Girl

Everybody's little girl
Because, because
I didn't want to hurt
Anyone the way I was.
Everybody's little girl
I could not choose.
If I did
Someone would lose.
Everybody's little girl
The answer came
Whenever asked
It was the same
"Everybody's little girl,"
I would reply.
I didn't want to make
Somebody cry.
Everybody's little girl
Because, because
"Everybody's little girl,"
That's what I was!

1952-53   Age 2 1/2

Alice Jane Risdon Stuckey

By the time Alice was two and a half, she had become everybody's little girl.

Excuses

Excuses you say
Oh, you make them too.
And I'm sorry to say
You're right, I sure do!
The building needs cleaning
But it's too far away.
Besides it would take
A good deal of the day!
We need a teacher
For that Bible class
But my eyes point downward
For fear they will ask.
The weary need visits
Just a few words of cheer
But surely they know
My time's very dear!

Fellowship

You need the strength of the church, my friend
If you ever hope to stay straight.
You cannot got it alone, my friend
And make it thru heaven's gate!
We need each other
If we're to stay strong.
I need you, my brother
I nccd to belong.
I need your acceptance
Not only when I'm on fire
But I especially need you
When I grow weary and tire.
The world is waiting
To draw you back in
And Satan is happy
When you fall into sin.
Come to the shelter
That fellowship offers.
Protected in love
From the world and its scoffers.

Fix My Mind

Lord, take me to where
Where you want me to be
That I might live.
My life for thee.
Though my mind knows
What you want me to do
My heart does not always
Care for you.
Help me, Lord
Stay my mind.
That I follow you
And not mankind!

Hang a Yellow Ribbon

Hang a yellow ribbon out.
A war is going on.
It's not in another land
Somewhere over yon.
The soldiers in this war span
From the young to very old.
Some are much too timid
And other's quite too bold.
The weapons they are using
Range from words to drug abuse.
A lack of discipline
And morals that are loose.
A lonely soldier weeps
And grieves in dark despair.
The wounds that he has suffered
Are very hard to bear.
Tie a yellow ribbon out.
The war is on your street.
I see it in the many eyes
Of the people that I meet.
Perhaps that yellow ribbon
Will cheer somebody's son
Give him strength to face the day
Until the battle's won.

Hang a yellow ribbon. A war is going on.

House Arrest

Jesus is in lock-up
He's under house arrest.
The only time he sees us
Is in our Sunday best!
We meet him Sunday morning
And bow before his throne.
But throughout the weekdays
He's sealed behind that stone!
How lonely must our Savior feel
Being locked inside those walls
While we run aimlessly through life
Breaking all his laws.
'Tis so selfish to keep him hid
While none the world can see
His beauty and his majesty
His love for you and me!

If You Knew Me

Would you like me
If you knew me
If you knew the things I did?
Would you like me
If you knew me
If you knew the things I said?
Things inside
I try to hide.
I cannot let them show.
No one must ever know.
Would you like me
If you knew me
How I talk behind your back?
Would you like me
If you knew me
And the character I lack?
I must hide the hard, cold facts.
Never, never to give in.
Covering up when I am lax.
Hoping none will see my sin!
Would you like me
If you knew me
If you followed me home at night?
Would you like me
If you knew me
If you saw the way I fight?

Always putting forth my best
It's so very hard
Fearful, I will fail the test
And be caught off guard!
Would you like me
If you knew me
And the hatred that I hold?
Would you like me
If you knew me
How my heart is bitter cold?
Other's joys I cannot share.
Alone, their sorrow, they must bear.
I cannot feel.
I just don't care!
Would you like me
If you knew me
If you knew me in my moods?
Would you like me
If you knew me
And the way I deal with foods?
Pills to kill my appetite.
Pills to make me sleep at night.
Pills to rid me of my dinner
Hoping I will look some thinner!
Would you like me
If you knew me
If you saw my sinful pride?
Would you like me

If you knew me
If I committed suicide?
The pain I feel within:
So deep, so dark
So hard to bear
Caused by a load of sin.
Would you like me
If you knew me
If you could see into my heart?
Would you like me
If you knew me
Or would you hate me from the start?
But God knew me and he loved me
And I bid him to come in.
He brought along the blood of Jesus
And washed away my sin.
I could not do it on my own.
I fought with Satan all alone.
I placed myself upon his throne.
It didn't work.
It never does.
We needn't worry, fret, or fuss
God is here for all of us.

I'll Get Thru

I may be having troubles
And my ego hurts a bit
But I'll get thru.
I may have done all I could
And finally up and quit
But I'll get thru.
I may be feeling like a failure
Cause I didn't stick it out
But I'll get thru.
I know that I can smile
While I'm walking down this road
Cause each and every mile
Someone's helping with my load.
He said he'll go with me
He's promised in his word.
I never have to be afraid
When I'm walking with my Lord.

Image

Craving for the world
around me.
Striving to fit in.
Grasping all
my eyes can see.
What if
it leads to sin?
Worried about
the outward shine.
Who will see
this house of mine?
Wanting to succeed
in life
No matter of
the stress and strife.
Short-sighted
by the here and now.
To fame and fortune
my knee I bow.
What seems important
day to day
Soon will end
and fade away.
Our life is just
a wisp in time.
To waste this day
would be a crime.
For Jesus suffered
much for me.
To bring me home
eternally.

In the Silence of Home

Always before
I've had my needs met
And there was nothing I've wanted
That I could not get!
But now there are times
That my money runs low
And I have to stay home
When I would rather go.
Now, God's not forsaken
His child and heir
For in the silence of home
I've found he is there!

Lazy Mary

"Lazy Mary, will you get up?"
My grandma sang to me.
"No, no, Grandma, I won't get up."
I would not hear her plea!
Down the road, my grandma walked
My cousin by her side.
She had a job for me to do
Instead in bed I lied.
Perhaps the Lord is pleading too
"Mary, will you get up?"
"I bled and died, that you might live."
"Mary, drink my cup!"

Nineveh

I don't want to go to Nineveh.
I'm living in a whale.
Instead of wishing my enemies good
I'd rather they would fail.
Does God have to rock my boat
To make me understand
It wasn't just for a chosen few
They pierced my Savior's hand?
I don't want to go to Nineveh.
I've much room to grow
But bit by bit and piece by piece
The Lord can change my soul!

Nothing Matters

Nothing matters
At least, nothing much!
—The little things
—The petty things
Nothing really matters!
It's nothing
If you're busy thinking
And fail to hear me speak.
It's nothing
If you haven't time
Because of the schedule that you keep.
It's nothing
If you lose your temper
And yell once in a while.
It's nothing
If you forget to praise
And share a cheerful smile.
The appreciation you failed to show
The apology you never made.
—It's nothing.
The helping hand you could have lent
The money you kept, instead of spent
—It's nothing!
The letter you never wrote
The hug you never gave.
—It's nothing.

The elderly person all alone
The soul that's needing saved.
—It's nothing!
I know you have your life to live
With all of its demands.
There's so little money to give
And so many greedy hands.
So many things get in the way
Of good we mean to do.
And soon our heart is hardened clay
I'm sorry, but it's true!
Yes, nothing much really does matter.
—The little things
—The petty things
A whole lot of nothings
Really do matter!

Return to the Throne

The green pastures above
And the valley below
He leads me on
Wherever I go.
Though life appears gloomy
And my hope grows dim
I know I can conquer
By turning to him.
Christ never forsakes me
Nor leaves me alone
But patiently waits
My return to the throne!

Roadblocks

Lord, if it's roadblocks that I need
Then, Lord, place them there for me.
I need your providential care
That I'll not bring offense to thee.
The flesh is weak
Temptations strong.
Left to myself
I do what's wrong
I've read your Word
I know what's right.
But I need your help
To win the fight!

Somebody Else's Tale

What is this game I'm playing?
How can it all be real?
Who is the person I'm portraying?
Doing a show for vaudeville.
Where did I read the book?
Where did I get the test?
It's a stranger in the mirror, when I look
Never knowing what to expect next!
It all seems so unreal.
It has to be a bad dream!
Hating the feeling I feel.
No help for me to redeem!
An actress up on a stage
A drama of my life.
Hopelessly filled with rag
Full of anger and strife.
I'm part of a horror show
One where I can't catch my breath.
It frightens and scares me so.
I feel my impending death!
It's somebody else's take.
This terrible escapade.
Enduring this living hell
And the hideous mess that I've made!

I am not weary.
I am not lost.
Cause Jesus Christ
Went to the cross.
Crucified
But now he lives.
I yield my life
And he forgives.

Swing with Me, Jesus

I knew a little girl
Who had a friend.
And everywhere she went
She would hold his hand.
She sang with Jesus
She swung with Jesus
And kept him by her side.
In everything she did
Her Lord was glorified.
Though no one else could see her friend
Or seemed to understand
She knew that he was by her side
Holding to her hand.
Swing with me, Jesus, once again
For I know you'll understand
That nothing can remove the pain
But the comfort of your hand!

Come Swing with Me. Alice at five years old.

The Ark

I've built me an ark
As Noah did.
People may ridicule
And people may kid.
But there's gonna be water
There's gonna be rain.
The world's full of suffering
The world's full of pain.
Through faith in his promise
I've entered the door.
I now walk with Jesus
I'll doubt him no more.
When this life is over
And the waters descend.
I'll step up in glory
With Jesus, my friend.

The Bully

Satan, that old bully
Came to my house the other day.
He knocked upon my door
And stood right in my way!
He knew I had decided
There were things that I must do
But he just up and popped in
Out of the clear blue.
He spoke up in my mind
And told me I was dumb
He brought along a friend of his
So they could poke some fun.
I began to grow fainthearted
And forget the power that I had.
He kept on throwing punches
And making me so mad.
But my Father had taught me
To stand my own ground.
Though some may not see him
He's always hanging around.
I looked that old devil
Right square in the face.
And pumped out Holy Scripture
Like a can of spraying mace!

The Chair

God, are you there
Sitting in the chair
While I run around
From here to there?
My life is so busy
From morning until night.
I've so many appointments.
My schedule is tight.
I say in the evening
I'll sit down with God
But before I know it
I feel my head nod.
Today, I'll make time
To sit in my chair.
I know you are waiting.
I know that you care!

The Rooster

The rooster and the devil
Must be friends, you know
Because he's always stalking me
Everywhere I go.
The rooster's always sneaking
Upon me in the yard
And if I am not careful
He catches me off guard.
Yes, I must be mindful
As I walk about each day
Because the rooster and the devil
Are never far away!

The Sirens of Odysseus

The sirens of the sea
They sing out to beckon me
"Come, sweet woman, come."
And I, in weakness, raise my head
Forgetting once that we were wed
And you and I are one!
The sirens with their music tease
Sweet melodies of rest and peace
"Come, sweet woman, come."
I must not linger here at sea
My heart and soul belong to thee.
My Father calls me home.

The Tiller of the Soil

Has a path been beaten
Through your field?
Has the ground been hardened
So it will not yield?
There is one who can till
The soil of your heart.
He is near to help
If you will do your part.
Are there friends that you choose?
Those who will fertilize your soul?
Will they nourish your heart?
And help you start to grow?

The Ugly Black Vessel

The ugliest black vessel
Laid buried below
A pile of rubble
In a deep, dark hole.
Somebody's treasure
Left in the clay
Forgotten, forsaken
In rotting decay.
So foul and offensive
That no one came near.
But from inside the vessel
I heard a faint tear.
What lay inside
I wanted to know.
A little step closer
I saw a slight glow.
I tried to remember
The day I said, "Yes."
His blood washed my sin
And cleaned up my mess.
My brother has wandered
Away from the fold.
In deep filthy dirt
He lies there so cold.

Won't someone remind him
Of joy simply forgot.
That ugly lack vessel
Just left there to rot.
My Heavenly Father
My Lord by his side.
He paid for my shame
Jesus Christ, crucified.
My Abba, my daddy,
Stands by the gate.
Fall in to his arms
Before it's too late!

Where Are the Tears?

Nowhere to flee
Nowhere to go
People surround me
But still, I'm alone.
Full of fears
But...
Where are the tears?
I hear the merry-making
Of voices nearby.
My heart is breaking
But I can't cry.
Laden and drear
But...
I can't shed a tear!
Others so gay
When I feel so blue.
I long for a way
To laugh with them too.
My heart—cold through the years,
But...
Where are the tears?
Pressures surround me
Like weights, I can't bear.
My burdens are heavy
Laden with care.
Longing for cheer
But...

I can't shed a tear.
My soul
And empty shell
Unwhole
A living hell.
Nothing seems clear
And…
I can't shed a tear.
Too tired to strive
To keep in the race.
Myself, I must drive
To keep up the pace.
All hope disappears
But…
Where are the tears?
Tired of trying
To rid my soul of gloom.
No hope for peace
When laid in the tomb.
I've tried for years
But…
I can't find the tears!
This is my goal
No matter how drained
To keep in control
And not to complain.
Eternal hell nears
But…

Where are the tears?
Outside, I seem so strong.
None else can see
Things are going wrong
Deep inside me.
No one ever hears
Inside…
I keep the tears!
The tears long have vanished
Replaced
By God's grace.
No longer that sadness
Not even a trace.
I gave my life to Jesus
And the sadness went away.
Because, now, when I am lonely
All I have to do is pray.
My abba, my Father, my daddy, my dad.
Comforts his daughter
and makes my heart glad.

Your Addictions and Mine

Although I do not understand
Just why you took a drink
Nor do I understand
The way you act and think
This one thing I do know
I have addictions all my own.
And Jesus said only those without sin
Should be casting that first stone.
And so we come together
Before the Father's throne,
Even though we are not perfect
We don't have to walk alone!
Yes, Christ hung upon the cross
To set the captive free.
Just when we think we can't go one
He's there for you and me!

3

Spiritual Comfort

Abba, Father, Daddy

Abba, Father, Daddy,
I come to you today
Knowing you are with me
At my work and play.
My little heart is yearning, Dad
To grow up big like you.
I want to show compassion, Lord
As I always see you do.
I have good intentions
And try to do my best
But some tasks are much too large for me
So I'll leave you do the rest.
If I follow closely, Dad
And imitate your way
I'll find that I am growing
A little bit each day.
Other kids are all alone
Their dads are never near.
So when evening shadows come
They have much to fear.
Abba, Father, Daddy
You're the best dad on the block.
You never go to sleep at night
You're with me round the clock!

Apologies

Does God demand an apology?
The way I do my child?
Does he sit and fuss and fume
And make him stew a while?
Does he refuse to hear his pleas
And let his child doubt?
When his child returns to him
Does he throw his child out?
Or is he waiting, as I have heard
With his arms spread wide and open?
Knowing we're sorry for our offense
Before the words have yet been spoken?

Beckoned to Prayer

We all have our trials
And burdens to bear.
Our world feels heavy
And full of care.
And though we know others,
This path have trod,
Our only help—our only hope
Is our Father, our God!
Heartaches come
And bend us so low
And seeking relief
We run to and fro.
But human answers
Can only bring pain
Unless we seek God
We seek in vain.
Though confused
And tattered and torn
I often feel used
And weary and worn
I know there is hope
And freedom in prayer.
My Heavenly Father
Beacons me there.

Betrayed

As they went to the garden
To pray and reminisce
Who would have thought
He'd be betrayed by a kiss?
And who would have thought
The friends by his side
Would be found sleeping
As he knelt there and cried?
Who would have thought
When his deepest need came
Those whom he loved
Would deny his name?
I stand here in awe
When I see how I live
That he's raising his eyes
Saying, "Father, forgive."

Empty Promises

Satan's lies sound so sweet
Tempting us to leave Jesus's feet!
He makes excuses for our behavior
So we gladly leave our Lord and Savior.
For one brief moment of sinful whim
We lose our chance to live with him.
I fight with all my strength and might
To defeat his lies, both day and night
But there is no power that lies within
My only hope is found in him.

Happy 49th

(Written for Bill on our 49th anniversary
March 29, 2018)

It's our day today
Even though you've gone away.
It's still "Our Day"
You were my husband.
I was your wife.
When we took our vows
We meant them for life.
The years came
And the years went.
I have no regrets.
They were years well spent.
Not always agreeing
But together, still the same.
Giving up singleness
For the sound of you name.
I knew the Lord
Put me in your life for a reason
But I had no idea why
Until the final season.
After a life time of trying
To do life on your own
God softened your heart
That seemed hard as stone.

"I want to follow Jesus,"
Were the words that you said.
Words I yearned to hear
Since the day we were wed!
Satan thought he had you.
But he was so wrong.
Your confession of Jesus
Our anniversary song.
Happy 49th anniversary in heaven, Bill.
I am so proud of you.

Love, Alice

Lost in the Sauce

Just a little pepper
In the middle of the sauce.
Nothing very special
The pepper felt so lost!
There was little time to notice her
With all those wondrous flavors.
And for all her mother knew
She could have been the neighbor's.
But it takes that little pepper
To make the sauce complete
For sauce without "the pepper,"
Is like chili without meat!
God, our Father, loves you.
He wants to see you win.
There's purpose in your being
There's good that lies within.
Jesus came from heaven
To die upon the cross.
He doesn't want that pepper
To get lost in the sauce!

One Greater Compliment

No greater compliment could be made
Than was made to me today.
When a lady came to visit
She said I had my grandma's way!
Now Grandma's ways were special
So generous, thoughtful, kind.
And when I think of Grandma
"Hard worker" comes to mind.
Always reading scripture
As she lay across her bed
Eager to share the Father's will
By teaching what he said.
This compliment I treasure.
A connection to the past
Proof that one small life in time
Spent well will surely last!
One greater compliment…
I long to hear folks say
Though Grandma's ways were special
"She has her Savior's way!"

Though Grandma's ways were special, she has her Savior's ways.

Wrap Your Arms around Me

Alice Stuckey
Pick me up
in your arms.
You're my refuge
You're my song.
When I'm down
Lift me up.
Keep me safe
Where I belong.
Wrap your arms around me, Jesus.
Show me that you care.
Wrap your arms around me, Jesus.
Remind me you are there.
When my burden grows heavy
I buckle from the load.
Take my hand.
Lead me back.
Set my feet
Upon the road.
Wrap your arms around me, Jesus.
Show me that you care.
Wrap your arms around me, Jesus.
Remind me you are there.
In my joy.
In my pain.
In the sunshine

And the rain.
Hold me close
To your breast.
Grant me peace
And grant me rest.
Wrap your arms around me, Jesus.
Show me that you care.
Wrap your arms around me, Jesus.
Remind me you are there.
There is love in your eyes.
There is see mercy in your face.
At the foot of the cross.
Is ever flowing grace.
Wrap your arms around me, Jesus.
Show me that you care.
Wrap your arms around me, Jesus.
Remind me you are there.

4

Poems on Death

A Mother's Child

Some mother's child died last night.
The car went off the road.
She had told him not to speed
But he didn't do as told.
"Get off my case,"
He yelled, as he hurried out the door.
And now the mother is alone.
She has a son no more!

A Mother's Last Thoughts

A daughter too young to be there
Two sons too young to know
One son trying to understand
Just why it should be so.
Their mother lies there so still
Her heart no longer beats.
She's aged from the suffering and pain.
She's grown thin from her cancerous death.
I wonder what her last thoughts were.
Most likely of her children
And husband.
Of the ones she would be leaving behind.
Was she afraid to pass through death's door?
Or was she looking for a peaceful rest?
Was she afraid to die so young?
Or did she feel it was for the best?
And I?
How would I feel, if God were to take me?
Would I be ready to die?
Or would I cling to the life I know?

All My Family That Used to Live

I'd give a million, to go back in time
If I had a million to give.
Just think of all the people, I'd find
All my family that used to live!
"Come on, Bessie," I'd say.
"Let's walk down to the beach."
"Remember, how in the sand I used to play?"
"Remember, when Flinch, you tried to teach me?"
Grandma Kuhl, I'd stop to see.
Together, we would play.
I'd share with you, my dolly.
Yes, we'd play the whole long day.
I'd stop at the rest home
To see Aunt Ollie.
I'd sit real nice in her room.
We'd have a good chat, by golly.
My grandpa, my brothers, and Aunt Mary
I'd see these people, I didn't know.
On my heart, their lives I'd carry.
Oh, how much my soul would glow!
I'd see Ma Delfing and Uncle Babe
I'd sit on Uncle Babe's knee.
I'd try my hardest to behave.
I'd be the sweetest I possibly could be.
I'd go see Doc and Uncle Tony
I'd be sure not to forget George Nagle.
Maybe, I'd drop in on Marie.
I'd go everywhere, I was able.

Then there was Dave and Mable Anthony
He was the only grandpa I knew.
I doubt he'd have accepted me
But I wish I'd know him too.
I'd spend the day with Mommy.
Everything, I'd want to know.
"What was I like when I was a baby?
"Tell me, where did we go?
"Tell me about when you were a kid.
"Tell me where you met Dad.
"Tell me about the things you did.
"Even when you were bad!
"You'll have to talk fast.
"Mommy, I want to know all about you.
"There's people that I could ask,
"But, I'm embarrassed to."
Grandma Risdon, I'd want to see most.
She'd listen to me play piano and sing.
"That's my Alice," she would boast.
Together, we would do creative things.
We'd take a walk back to Sugar Creek
Maybe pick berries on the way.
We'd play statues; red light-green light; or hide 'n' seek.
I'd beg her to let me play in the hay.
Maybe, I'd straighten her newspaper cupboard
Maybe, her wash, we'd do
Maybe, she'd read me a story about my Lord.
Maybe, she'd sew me a dress, all new.
"Grandma," I'd say, "it's been fun today.
"Tomorrow, I'd like to come too.
"Today, and my whole life through."

All My Family That Used to Live

So many wonderful people pass through our lives and on to eternity. As they pass, a piece of them rubs off on us and attaches itself to our hearts. No one can ever take their spot, for whenever we think of them, we feel warm all over.

Grandfather's cousin, Bessie Sherod, was an old-maid schoolteacher, who lived in my fantasy home near the lake. Someday I shall have to write more about this fine lady!

Great-Grandma Kuhl died when I was four. And Aunt Ollie, Grandfather's sister, was Daddy's rich aunt, who died in the poor house.

Grandpa died when I was two, and Aunt Mary, Daddy's sister, died when I was one.

I never knew my brothers, Thomas Wayne and James Michael, for they died as babies, but I grieved their loss perhaps much more than one could imagine. They were the brothers I never knew. They were the missing link to my life.

Ma Delfing, my stepmom's mother, and Uncle Babe, her twin? Dave, my stepmom's real father? My stepmom's family had their place too. Doc and her cousin George were all just like my kin.

Marie Gatton, our Amherst neighbor, couldn't have been much past forty when a brain tumor left her sons and husband without their mother.

And then, of course, two of the most important people in my life, my mother, who was taken with cancer, when I was three (she was thirty-two). And my dear, dear Grandma.

Do you have someone you're missing today? Look into your heart. Draw back those times and feel their closeness once again!

I would visit all my family that used to live.

All Too Few

My child, I love you
So often I say.
I had a child
But he went away.
I remember how he smiled.
And how his eyes shined so bright.
He's no longer here.
He walks in your light.
My heart yearns
Hard and longs for you.
The days we had
Were all too few!

Although We've Never Met

I feel we're friends
Although we've never met.
To bad your life had to end
But people don't forget.
Everywhere I go
I hear a praising phrase.
Your name, they always know
With pleasant words, they recall the days.
"She was the nicest lady."
"She never had anything bad to say."
"She was very close to me."
"We were sisters, in a way."
They tell me how things would have been
If you were living still.
People write of you with their pen.
"Ma did this," I hear from Bill.
Some days, I close my eyes
And just pretend
nobody ever dies
And you are with us all again!

Bedtime Stories

Before I was old enough to know what death was
Death was!
Before I knew what life was
It was no more!
While still an infant in the crib
Death reached its ugly claws through the bars
And snatched life's breath from those
Who should have been mine!
Death made himself my bedtime stories
With memories of the Grandmother
Who grieved her own losses.
She was mine—at least for now.
Death would patiently wait
An opportune time
To snatch this one, he left behind.
Then, too, she would be
A bedtime story of
Another grieving her losses.

Camping Out

It's time to tear the tent down.
I've been camping out too long.
It's time to tear the tent down
And go home where I belong.
The torrents of the welfare lines
"The world owes me a living."
"Do what you can to get ahead."
Always taking, never giving!
Garbage filters through the camp.
Greed lies everywhere.
I'll not rest at peace again,
'Til I rest over there.
Yes, it's time to tear the tent down.
I've been camping out too long.
It's time to tear the tent down
And go home where I belong!

Some days I just close my eyes and pretend.

Changes

What used to be
Is no more.
I once was rich
But now I'm poor.
Though I have
Much goods and money
I've lost my love
My lifelong "Honey."
The man I knew
For all these years
Knowing this
Brings forth the tears.
I can't imagine
What lies ahead.
My heart is heavy
So full of dread.

Christmas 2014

Home with Jesus
That's where you are
Home with Jesus
Not very far.
It won't be long
'Til I join you, son.
I'll see you again
When this life is done.
Until that day I'll remember
The time that we shared.
The way that you loved
And the way that you cared.
Merry Christmas
Love, Mom.

Christmas Past

Sherry's dead.
She's in the ground.
We buried her
Outside of town.
Yet, it seems like yesterday
That I heard Sherry say
"I love you, Aunt Alice
I always will."
"And I also love
my Uncle Bill."
Who would have thought
That Christmas past
Would have been
Dear Sherry's last?

Feel

If I could feel,
Like others do
Then maybe I
Could grieve for you.
If I could cry
And let it out
If I could scream
Get mad and shout
If I could reach
The pain inside
Then I would have
Already cried.

Gone

I reach.
I search.
I wonder
I remember.
I miss.
I worry I will forget.
I want to talk to you
Once again.
I want to hold you
Once again.
Just a quiet word.
A hug
To hear
"I love you, Mom."
But all is silence.
No word.
Only memories.
Memories of then.
Not now.
Now I am alone.
I have no one.
You are gone.

Granddaughter of Ruth

It's a story of love
And a story of truth
Of a little girl
Granddaughter of Ruth.
It seems a fairytale
As I look back
The farm in the dale
Stone house by the track.
Walks back the lane
To Sugar Creek
Playing Mother-may-I?
Or hide-and-seek.
The slower life
The simple life
A time to sense God's beauty.
The purer life
The serving life
With time to do one's duty!
But years marched on
And Grandma died.
We buried her out
In the countryside.
But Grandma lives one
She will not be still.
She lives in the heart
Of this little girl.

Here on Loan

You entrusted him to me, for a little while
To raise, to love, to guide.
You let me teach him.
Of your love and our Savior…crucified.
You equipped him with
a brave, strong heart
Full of loyalty, truth, and honor.
You purposed him to
touch his world for your glory, Father.
Cloaked with God's full armor
Christ follower, disciple
witness, scholar.
Charming, polite
My gallant knight.

Home for Christmas

Home for Christmas
Yes, that's where I'd like to be
Sitting next to Grandma
Beside our tiny tree.
Home for Christmas
As I travel though the years
When life was much too peaceful
For such a thing as tears!
Home for Christmas
The road has long been closed
Tangled in the underbrush
Of all life's cares and woes!
Grandma no longer
Sits in her rocking chair
In fact the house where we once lived
Is no longer there!
Christmas is a lonely time
Sitting here alone.
Yes, home for Christmas
If the truth be known
I'd rather spend this Christmas Day
In my heavenly home!

Grandma lives on in the heart of the little girl.

Missing

I look into the future
And I wonder what's in store.
Life passes so quickly
Now that I'm sixty-four.
Yesterday was full of dreams.
So many wants to do.
But since the day you journeyed home.
Those dreams have died with you.
Oh, that I could feel the love you felt.
The peace that shone each day.
Your twinkling eyes and lovely smile
You always gave away.
I am happy you're with the Lord.
I'm relieved you're free of pain.
But something will always be missing
Until we meet again.

My Grandma Was Real

It seems so long ago now
When I was a little girl.
Though I have but memories
I know my grandma was real.
The time on the farm
And the fun that we had.
I cherish the memories
With Grandma and Dad.
Would that I could
Bring my grandma back
And visit that lady
In the house by the track.
But life doesn't permit
Us to bring back the dead.
It only commands
That we move on ahead.
So my thank you to Grandma
Must be in the love that I give
My duty to God
And the life that I live.

One Year

A year in heaven
What's it like?
To walk with streets?
So shining bright?
To gaze upon
The Savior's face,
To fully know
His saving grace?

Power behind Faith

They say his faith
Shone through twinkling eye
The smile on his face
While others cry.
They gave him credit
For a faith that was strong
For trusting Jesus
When all seemed so wrong.
For truly it wasn't
This man who lay there.
It was the power of love
And answered prayer.
Jesus in others
The comfort of song
The body of Christ
To which we belong.

Psalm 137 in Light of Death
Beside Brian's deathbed, I wept.
As I thought of life as it was.
We put away our dreams
As we resigned ourselves
To his impending death.
There would be no more bounce in his step
As he danced to the music.
Satan has robbed him of his song.

I cherish the memories with Grandma and Mom.

Ready to Go

I've picked myself up
And I'm feeling much better.
I won't make excuses
Like this winter weather.
When I'm missing my loved ones
I find myself down.
I'll get n my car
And drive into town.
Many are lonely
This time of the year
Perhaps I can cheer them
By just being near
God's plan for me in this season
I may not know.
I've zipped up my coat
I'm ready to go.

Satan May Try

Satan believed he's robbed his song
But the melodies and tones sing through his heart.
Disease has captured the tones of his mouth
But cannot still the song in his soul.
Disease has sapped the strength of his legs
But still he runs the race with valor.

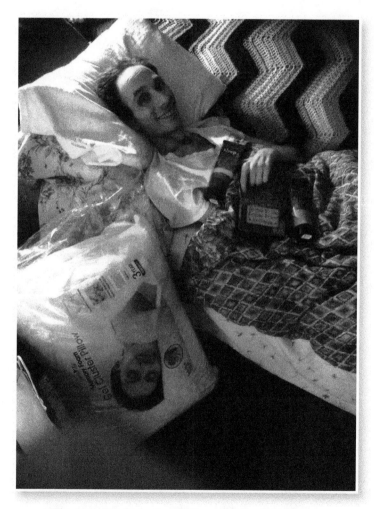

They say his faith shown through twinkling eyes.

Soothing Balm

The solace of my grief
Is your belief
In the Heavenly Father's love.
Knowing that your suffering's done
Resting in the heavenly sun
With our God above.
Knowing that you stood the test.
Knowing you have peace and rest.
Is my soothing balm.
Knowing things won't be the same
But that you called on Jesus's name
Brings me peace and calm.

Tears of Joy

Tears for the father
I came to know too late.
I came to hug only at the last.
For the memories
For the dad I can't visit.
Tears for the dad
I never could have confided in.
Who until I grew old
Never knew I existed.
Tears for the father-in-law
Who loved his grandson.
Who loved his son
And who, in his own way, loved me.
Gone so long
He seems like a story.
Tear for my son's dad
Who doesn't know God
Who thinks that his is God
For his lostness
Because when his son dies
He has nothing to hold on to.
Tears for those three men
Fathers in my life
But...
Fatherless in their spirits.
Tears for my son
Wanting to go home to
His Father in heaven.

To rest in his true home
To see his elder brother, Jesus.
Tears for him never seeing his father
His grandfathers
Giving credit and love to the
One true God.
Tears for I am selfish
And would keep my son back for myself.
I would not let him go.
I would beg and plead
With my Father not to take him from me
When Christ, his big brother
Has already prepared a mansion for him.
He has a new body waiting for him.
He has a ballroom in this mansion
Where he can cha-cha
Around the throne of his heavenly father
With new strong legs.
He can lift his new strong arms in praise
As his sings out clearly.
"Father, Father,"
Tears of joy
Know my son knows his Father
And I have nothing to fear.
Written for Brian Stuckey on
Father's Day, June 16, 2013
By his mother, Alice Jane Stuckey

God Are You There?

God, are you there
Sitting in the chair
While I run around
From here to there?
My life is so busy
From morning until night.
I've so many appointments.
My schedule is tight.
I say in the evening
I'll sit down with God
But before I know it
I feel my head nod.
Today, I'll make time
To sit in my chair.
I know you are waiting.
I know that you care!

The Closet

I've emptied out your closets.
The coats are for the poor.
God's called you home to heaven
And you don't need them anymore.
I take a shirt off the hanger
And hold it to my breast.
A smile comes across my face
Remembering how you dressed.
I hold your hat in my hand.
I pull a suit off the rack.
I have to face the truth.
You're never coming back.

The Man He Was

I scarce believe the man I see
This stranger who's come home to me.
This man who is but a shell
Of one I knew so very well.
He tries so hard to act the same.
I turn my head to hide the pain
Of memories of the man he was
Sweet memories of the two of us!

The Pew

In the pew behind the preachers
Stands a very special man.
Sometimes I see you singing there
At least I think I can!
No, it's not my son who stands
His arm raised in the air.
He's gone home to Jesus
And life seems so unfair.
But God had the best in mind
When he took you from that pew.
Tonight you dance with Jesus
In a body that's brand new!
Love,
Mom

The Porch

I sit on the empty porch.
I swing on the empty swing.
I mouth the words to a song
I used to hear you sing.
The porch was built just for you.
It took too long to do.
The task was much to large.
The hours were too few.
Now you're gone forever.
I sit here all alone
Knowing that you'll never
No, never come back home.

The Visit

I've come to visit
You today
I have so much
I want to say.
Remember how we sang
When we were in the car?
We nudged dad's heart just a crack
And left that door ajar.
The bits and pieces
Of the word
As we talked
Dad overheard.
Because of all
Our prayers and tears
His heart was softened
Through the years.
I saw him humbled
As he confessed.
I jumped for joy
I felt so blessed.
You must not cry
For us down there.
Dad's safely home.
God answered prayer.

Sweet memories of the two of us.

Too Soon

I lost my companion
When God took you home.
Your journey had ended
For you were full grown.
You mature much too quickly
For my mind to grasp.
God, in his wisdom
Said you finished your task.
Some jobs go quickly
And some jobs go slow
But when your purpose has ended
Then you must go.
Your assignment completed.
Your purpose fulfilled.
Now you're in heaven
God's glory revealed!

Treasured Memories

The experiences throughout the years
The hope, the love, the sweat, and tears
Now gives me strength to face my fears.
Since the day
You went away
I lean on God.
He is my stay.
The love I feel
I cannot measure.
But they are mine
To hold and treasure.
Memories here
Cannot compare
What will be
When I meet you there!

What I want for Christmas

I want the joy for living.
I want the desire for giving.
I want to wake each day
Remembering first to pray.
I want the peace that passes understanding.
I want his love to fill my heart.
I want a passion for my Savior
That filled me at the start.
I want my life to make a difference.
I want this day to be used for you.
When someone's care is lifted.
I want it to be your face they view!

You Are Not There

Needing to talk
Needing to share.
Trying to reach you
But you are not there.
I look in the office.
I look in your chair.
I look for your bed
To ruffle your hair.
This room has changed
And you are not there.
Your place at the table
Is empty and bare.
This isn't a fable.
You are not there!
You feast in his presence
It seems so unfair.
But if I am truthful
I'm glad you are there!

5

Poems on Depression

Just Wonderful

Whenever anyone asked her how she was
She'd reply
"Just wonderful."
Just wonderful because
"Just wonderful," was all they wanted to hear.
She knew they didn't want to know
Of the struggles she faced each day.
"How are you?" was just something
They felt they ought to say.
"Just wonderful."
Though she really ached inside.
"Just wonderful."
The perfect place to hide.

A Need for Silence

Do I know how to master the art of silence?
I need to.
No one really cares.
What I have to say is just noise.
I am nothing.
My story is nothing.
My life is nothing.
I used to be a friend
A wife
A mother
My friends have left.
My husband is lost.
My son is dead.
I am nothing.
I need to withdraw.
I need to isolate.
I need to be silent.

All Hope Lost

Tired of trying
To find the right answer.
Feels like I'm dying
Of a deadly cancer!
Laden with care
I can't keep up the pace
Getting no where
I'm standing in place.
Too much time spent
Trying to get well
Can't make a rent
In this living hell.
Intellectually knowing
The things I should do.
But while others are glowing
I'm sad and so blue.
Feeling aloft
From those who surround me.
Being cut off
My problems abound me.
Looking everywhere
But no solution to be found.
Life is empty and bare
Even with others around.

All hope lost
For any remission.
Too high the cost
To change my condition.
So I go through life
From day to day
Accepting this strife
As the only way.

Alone with God

It's night now.
And nowhere to go.
All have gone
To their homes
And loved ones.
And I?
I am alone!
No
Not alone.
I have my loved ones.
But I'm restless.
They are here
Beside me.
Yet I feel
Isolated.
Yes
Alone!
Alone with myself.
Alone with my thoughts.
Alone with my God!
I can't flee
From God at night.
I can't deny
The sins of the day.
I don't want to be alone.
Not with God!

I can't fool him.
I can't hide my heart.
I can't pretend
To be
What I am not!
I'm afraid
At night.
Afraid of the only one
Who knows
The only one who
Has the power.
I'm afraid
Of the truth.
I'm afraid
Of God!

An Honorable Position

We all have our place in life
A job we're called to do
But so often we feel the strife
Just trying to get through.
I feel that I am better
Just one step up upon the scale
And when you get that promotion
I can't see how I could fail!
Why, I've been around much longer!
My dedication has proven true.
My skills are so much stronger,
So why have they chosen you?
Why, I'm the one who is here
Each and every day!
I'm not afraid to work hard
And get a dirty hand.
Oh, Lord, please help me
As I pray
I just don't understand!
Not everyone can lead the pack.
We need those who can serve.
Serving is a humbling act
And honor I deserve!

Death of the Molester

I don't know how I feel:
Relief he'll never touch me
Or another again?
Relief I won't
Have to watch him
Die in pain?
Sadness?
For the loss
I feel?
For what
Might have been
Real?
Guilt?
For blaming him
For his sin
Facing the fact
I, too, sinned with him.

Drifting Out to Sea

Give me a hug
Please, somebody, give me a hug.
They feel so good to me.
Give me a hug
Quick, somebody, give me a hug
I'm drifting out to sea.
A hug makes me feel all warm
To know that someone's there.
Showing with their outstretched arm
Just how much they care.
Give me a hug
Please, give me a hug.
They feel so good to me.
Give me a hug
Quick, somebody, give me a hug.
I'm drifting out to sea.

6

Silly Poems

My Ugly Christmas Sweater

I love my Christmas sweater.
It has everything I need.
It really is so much better
Than yours that's made of tweed.
Christmas rush brings so much stress
And worry how much I'll gain.
With the strainer on my chest
My fears go down the drain.
The bells I wear upon my sleeves
Let people know I'm coming
Is case they cannot hear
The joyful songs I'm humming.
Sometimes I get a little crazy
But that's really not a factor.
That's why I carry on my top
My very own nutcracker.
If you see me with my spatula
Looking around the room
I may be looking for my bachelor
Because I want to spoon.
The noodle cutter is
To cut me down to size.
Just give me a little slap.
If I act too wise.

In case I need shut up
I brought along a bottle cap
If that doesn't work
With the boot give me a zap.
If my mouth keeps running
Just use the water bottle stopper.
If that does not work
Throw me in the nearest hopper.
I brought my own air freshener
In case I make a stink.
And my little bush clean things up
Quicker than you can blink.
With all these tools that my sweater conceals
There may be some sweater stealers.
So if anyone has that in mind
Just use my potato peeler.

Good Old Days

I hear people reminisce of the good old days.
I'm here to report, they had a few frays.
Man hasn't always gotten water from the sink
He used a bucket and dipper to attain a drink.
He pulled the water up from the well
Using a chain and some kind of pail.
After a few years, the bottom grew weak
And naturally the pail would leak.
And in the winter, when it snowed
They had to clean it away, all the cold.
Or what if the bucket come off the chain?
Getting it back would be quite a pain!
Of course, he wouldn't use a large amount
I know the buckets, he'd be sure to count.
If you wanted your water hot
You'd first need to heat it in some kind of pot.
Do they mean to tell me their water they'd rather be fetchin'
Then getting a drink from the sink in the kitchen?
Or what of the inside commode?
Do they mean they'd rather go out in the cold?
To stumble down the path in the middle of the night?
To be scarred by a rat and run in fright?
When it's warm, oh, the odor!
And you wish it were colder!
Spiders and bugs, you're always sure to find.
It may be their idea of comfort, but it's surely not mine.
Someone has to clean it out.
They've forgotten that, no doubt!
I've not experienced being without other stuff
But I can imagine it must have been rough.

The Case of the Missing Teeth

They were just a little piece.
Meant to fit tight above my chin.
But because they hurt too much
I couldn't keep them in.
Asked myself, "What could have happened?"
I searched high and I searched low.
Remembered putting them in a napkin.
Where on earth did they go?
Asked, "Jesus, help me find them.
"You know right where they are."
I left then with the cashier
When I used my credit card!

The Wheelchair

Alice got run over by a wheelchair
coming down from upstairs yesterday
You ask me where Alice was
When that darn wheel chair got away.
She didn't think the wheel chair was that heavy
She thought she could hold it backing down.
But before she fully knew what had hit her
She found herself buried on the ground.
All she really wanted was to find out
If a wheelchair could fit the bathroom door.
Fifteen steps and seconds later
Alice laid sprawled out upon the floor!

It only took eight and a half years for my husband
to put running water in the house.

Afterward

All Glory to God my faithful Father, my forever friend, who knew when I was in my mother's womb

> For you created my inmost being;
> you knit me together in my mother's womb
> and who has never left me nor forsaken me.
> (Ps 139:13, NIV)

> Keep your lives free from the love of money
> and be content with what you have, because God
> has said,
>> "Never will I leave you;
>> never will I forsake you." (Heb. 13:5, NIV)

I know I can trust him with my very being. He is the lover of my soul.

> For I am convinced that neither death nor
> life, neither angels nor demons, neither the pres-
> ent nor the future, nor any powers, neither height
> nor depth, nor anything else in all creation, will
> be able to separate us from the love of God that is
> in Christ Jesus our Lord. (Rom. 8:38–39, NIV)

Feed the Birds

Did you feed my birds?

"Feed the birds," I kept hearing someone say. "Do you hear me? Feed my birds."

Was that my husband speaking to me?

"Did you feed my birds?"

Yes, it very well could have been Bill. So often he had asked me, "Did you feed my birds? Do they miss me? Come, look at my birds! How many are there? They depend on me."

No, it wasn't Bill. It was a question. No, not a question, it was a command. It was God speaking. He was reminding me about Bill's love for his animals. All animals.

God has a purpose for all of us. And I know his grand purpose for Bill was to glorify him. He did just that the day he gave his life to Jesus just six weeks before he died.

I happen to believe God has many purposes for us throughout our lives here on earth.

Caring for God's creatures was one of many he had for Bill.

Bill was gone now. Perhaps one of the jobs he has in heaven is feeding the birds. I like to picture him doing just that.

But what about the birds still fluttering about in the trees just outside my window and in the valley and woods behind my house? Who is going to take care of the birds now?

"Feed my birds."

It was a dual request. One from Bill and another from God. Yes, I would feed the birds.

> Look at the birds of the air; they do not sow or reap or store away in barns, and yet your heavenly Father feeds them. Are you not much more valuable than they? (Matt. 6:26, NIV)

Bill's Story

Anyone who knew our son, Brian, knows he always had a good story to tell. Brian's faithful witness through the horrible disease of ALS was faced and nobly carried out with honor and love—both for his Lord and Savior and for his friend.

If anyone would have told me Brian's story would be trumped by his daddy, I wouldn't have believed it. But, happily, I am pleased to tell you it is so.

For those who knew Bill casually, you probably thought he was a Christian. But if you knew him personally, you would have known how foolish he believed Christianity to be.

As Brian lay dying, he begged his daddy to believe. Bill refused.

You can only imagine my surprise when, on October third of this year, I received a call for the hospital, tell me, "Your husband asked me to call you and tell you his birthday is tomorrow and he wants to be baptized."

When I walked into the visitor's room, Bill told me, "You're too late. God and the devil were fighting over me. I had an appointment with God. He said I had to be baptized by my birthday. I had to be immersed."

I assured him his birthday was tomorrow. I was not too late. The devil just wanted him to believe he was too late so he wouldn't be baptized.

"But you had to bring one of your men with you," he protested.

I assured him Jay was on his way.

When Jay arrived, he talked with Bill and found him to be lucid that day.

When Jay asked him if he believed that Jesus was the son of God and that he died for his sins and did he want to follow God the rest of the days, he didn't say yes. He didn't nod. He very clearly said, "I want to follow Jesus."

After Bill's confession of faith, Jay sprinkled him. "In the name of the Father and of the Son and of the Holy Spirit."

The following days were a mixture of lucidity and not. But on the good days, he told myself and others of his belief.

Bill kept telling me he had to do it over. He had to be baptized again. He had to be immersed. So on October 27, friends and family watched as our longtime friend and preacher, John Kerr, Pastor Dave Brown, and Brian's friend, Mike Straight helped Bill as he entered the watery grave of baptism to be raised in Christ a new creation.

I confess, I had given up on Bill. We have been married forty-eight years. Bill was seventy-three. Bill had Alzheimer's, PTSD, bipolar, and vascular dementia. In my mind, God had allowed Bill to harden his heart. In my humanness, I had forgotten what we read in Philippians. With God, all things are possible. God is not willing that any should be lost. He is patient and longsuffering. It was not too late for Bill.

And it is not too late for you. At Brian's funeral four years ago, I asked the question, Brian's friend an former youth, Nick, asked Brian just before he died, "How can I not believe?"

It wasn't too late for Bill and it isn't too late for you. If Brian and Bill were here today, they would be asking you the same. "Please, won't you believe?"

November 23, 2017

God is good.
The devil is bad.
God is going
to save me.

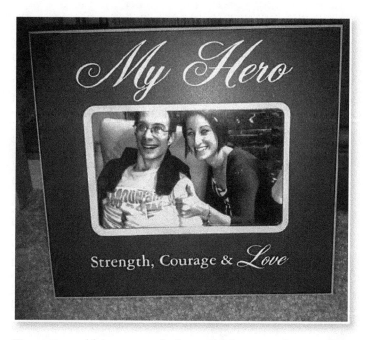

You purposed him to touch the world for your glory, Father.

About the Author

Alice Jane Stuckey began writing at the age of thirteen, after being given a writing assignment to compose a poem.

After her son, Brian, passed away from ALS at the age of forty-two, December 29, 2013, she published his memoir, *Walking Brian Home, One Man's Story of Faith in the Face of Death*.

She has found writing to be a way to process life's events and to meditate on God's blessings, purpose, strength, and guidance as she travels through life.

Though not yet published, Alice has manuscripts about growing up on a dairy farm in the 1950s, living through the horror of sex abuse, sharing life with her husband, a Vietnam vet who suffered from PTSD, and years of prayer journals which she references while writing.

Alice had the pleasure of recording her daddy's memories of growing up in Vermilion, Ohio, from 1913 to 2008. She hopes someday to be able to share these stories with others.

Since her husband, Bill's, passing with Alzheimer's and vascular dementia, on Thanksgiving 2017, Alice has kept herself active in her church and volunteering for hospice. She hopes to share the love and comfort that God so graciously has given her.

CPSIA information can be obtained
at www.ICGtesting.com
Printed in the USA
BVHW091914140619
551007BV00004B/10/P